DOMINOES

Troy

QUICK STARTER   250 HEADWORDS

OXFORD
UNIVERSITY PRESS

Great Clarendon Street, Oxford, OX2 6DP, United Kingdom

Oxford University Press is a department of the University of Oxford.
It furthers the University's objective of excellence in research, scholarship,
and education by publishing worldwide. Oxford is a registered trade
mark of Oxford University Press in the UK and in certain other countries

© Oxford University Press 2013

The moral rights of the author have been asserted

First published in Dominoes 2013

2019 2018 2017 2016

10 9 8 7 6 5 4 3 2

ISBN: 978 0 19 424970 6   Book
ISBN: 978 0 19 463909 5   Book and Audio Pack

Printed in China

This book is printed on paper from certified and well-managed sources

ACKNOWLEDGEMENTS

Cover photo: iStockPhoto (Greek helmet in sand/Eduard Andras).

Illustrations by: Laura Tolton/Advocate Art

The publisher would like to thank the following for the permission to reproduce photographs: Corbis
p.25 (Ruins of ancient Roman baths, Antonine Baths, Carthage, UNESCO World Heritage
Site, Tunis, Tunisia, North Africa, Africa/Stuart Black/Robert Harding World Imagery);
Robert Harding World Image p.24 (Archeological site of Troy, ruins of the ancient city of
Troy, Turkey, Europe/R&D VALTERZA/Cubo Images).

DOMINOES

Series Editors: Bill Bowler and Sue Parminter

Troy

Retold by Bill Bowler

Illustrated by Laura Tolton

Bill Bowler studied English Literature at Cambridge University
and mime in Paris before he became an English language
teacher, trainer, and materials writer. He loves the theatre,
cinema, history, art – and travelling. He also enjoys reading
books and writing poetry in his free time. Bill lives in Alicante
with his wife, Sue Parminter, and their three children. This
Dominoes retelling of the Trojan War story is based on Greek
and Roman versions of the tale.

OXFORD
UNIVERSITY PRESS

Story Characters

Priam Hecuba Cassandra Hector Paris

TROJANS

Agamemnon Menelaus Helen Odysseus Patroclus Peleus Achilles

GREEKS

Zeus Hera Aphrodite Athena Hermes Thetis Eris

GODS AND GODDESSES

Contents

BEFORE READING

1 **Write the number of a place name on the map next to each sentence.**

   a The Trojan king Priam and his family live here. ☐
   b Paris lives here, south of Troy, when he is a boy. ☐
   c The great Greek king Agamemnon is from here. ☐
   d Menelaus is from here, in the south of Greece. ☐

2 **Choose the words to complete these sentences. Use the character page to help you**

   a Paris is Priam and Hecuba's *brother / son*.
   b Cassandra and Hector are Paris's *children / sister and brother*.
   c Menelaus and Agamemnon are *brothers / father and son*.
   d Achilles is Peleus and Thetis's *son / grandfather*.

3 **Match the sentence endings with the names. For Greeks at the time of the story, these are true sentences.**

   a The River Styx ☐   **i** … is the home of the Greek gods.
   b Mount Olympus ☐   **ii** … is near the country of dead people. Its dar
                                         waters can stop people dying.

Everything begins when Priam is the **King** of Troy, and Hecuba is his **queen**.

At first, things go well for them. They have a daughter – Cassandra – and later, a son – Hector. Then, after some more years, they have a second son. His name is Paris.

But when this child arrives, Hecuba is not happy.

'What's wrong?' Priam asks.

'I'm afraid,' Hecuba answers. 'I see Troy **in flames** years from now – because Paris brings **disaster** to us.'

Priam takes away his young son fast.

king the most important man in a country

queen the wife of a king

in flames red and hot with fire

disaster a very bad thing

He speaks quietly to one of his men, **Agelaus**. 'Take this child into the **mountains**. He must die there.'

So Agelaus takes Paris to Mount Ida. But he cannot kill the young boy there.

'You can live here with me. And help with the **sheep** when you're older,' Agelaus says.

He gives the child to one of the women in his country house. Then he goes back to Troy. He gives a dead dog's **heart** to Priam and says, 'My king, your son is dead. Here's his heart.'

'Good work, Agelaus,' Priam smiles.

READING CHECK

Choose the correct words to complete these sentences.

a Priam and Hecuba are the King and Queen of _Troy_ / _Greece_.

b Their oldest child is _Cassandra_ / _Hector_.

c Hecuba _is_ / _isn't_ happy with her second son, Paris.

d He can bring _wonderful things_ / _disaster_ to Troy, she sees.

e Priam gives the child to Agelaus, one of his _men_ / _brothers_.

f 'He must _live_ / _die_ on the mountains,' Priam says.

g Agelaus takes Paris to Mount _Olympus_ / _Ida_.

h He leaves the boy with a _woman_ / _man_ in his country house.

i He gives a dead _dog's_ / _cat's_ heart to Priam.

j Priam _cries_ / _smiles_ when Agelaus says, 'Your son is dead.'

GUESS WHAT

What happens in the next chapter? Tick three sentences.

a Paris helps with Agelaus's sheep. ☐

b Suddenly, Agelaus dies one day. ☐

c Paris goes back to Troy and meets King Priam. ☐

d Priam is angry with Paris, and he kills his son. ☐

e The Greek king Peleus takes a goddess to be his queen. ☐

f The gods come from Olympus and eat at Peleus's house. ☐

Chapter 2 The golden apple

shepherd a man or boy who looks after sheep

honest saying things that are true

god an important being who never dies and who decides what happens in the world

goddess a woman god

marry to make someone your wife or husband

wedding the time when two people marry

disagreement when people think differently and cannot all say 'yes' to one thing

So Paris lives on Mount Ida. When he is young, he helps with Agelaus's sheep. He is a wonderful **shepherd** boy.

'And he's very **honest**, too,' Agelaus says. Soon everybody in the country knows about Agelaus's son – the honest young shepherd.

〜〜〜〜〜〜〜〜〜〜

In Greece at the same time, King Peleus of Thessaly is happy. He asks the **gods** and **goddesses** from Mount Olympus to his house. Why? Because he is **marrying** Thetis, a young sea goddess.

Peleus asks all the gods to the **wedding**. But he forgets one of the goddesses. Her name is Eris. She is the goddess of **disagreements**.

After the wedding, Peleus, Thetis, and the gods and godesses sit at a long table.

4

'I'm hungry. Let's eat,' Zeus, the King of Olympus, says to everyone there.

Just then, Eris arrives.

'Goddesses, here's something for you,' she cries.

She quickly puts a **golden** apple on the table. Then, with an angry laugh, she leaves.

Hera, the Queen of Olympus, takes the apple in her hand. 'I can read something on it,' she says.

'What?' Aphrodite, the love goddess, asks.

golden made of gold, an expensive yellow metal

Hera looks at it carefully. 'For the most beautiful,' she reads.

'But who's that?' Athena, Zeus's daughter, asks.

'Let's ask Zeus,' Hera laughs. She quickly gives the golden apple to him.

'Hmm. I can't say,' Zeus answers. 'We need help from an honest man, I think.'

'Listen!' Hermes cries. 'There's a very honest young shepherd on Mount Ida. Let's ask him.'

'All right,' Zeus says. He puts the golden apple in the **messenger** god's hand.

At once, Hermes takes the goddesses Hera, Athena, and Aphrodite to Mount Ida.

messenger
someone who
takes news
to people

READING CHECK

Are these sentences true or false? Tick the boxes.

		True	False
a	Paris helps Agelaus with his dogs on Mount Ida.	☐	☑
b	Paris is a good shepherd and an honest young man.	☐	☐
c	King Peleus marries Thetis, a sun goddess.	☐	☐
d	He asks all the gods to his house when he marries.	☐	☐
e	He forgets one goddess, Eris.	☐	☐
f	Eris arrives and puts a red apple on the table.	☐	☐
g	She laughs happily when she leaves.	☐	☐
h	The apple is for the most beautiful Greek goddess.	☐	☐
i	Hermes takes Hera, Athena, and Aphrodite to Mount Ida.	☐	☐

GUESS WHAT

What happens to Paris in the next chapter? Tick a box to finish each sentence.

a He gives the golden apple to …

   1 ☐ Hera.

   2 ☐ Athena.

   3 ☐ Aphrodite.

b He visits …

   1 ☐ Mount Olympus.

   2 ☐ Troy.

   3 ☐ Greece.

c He meets …

   1 ☐ Helen.

   2 ☐ Priam.

   3 ☐ Thetis.

Chapter 3 Who is the best?

Soon Hermes and the goddesses meet Paris.

Hermes gives Eris's apple to the young shepherd. He tells Paris all about it.

'Now look and please tell us: who is the most beautiful goddess of them all?' he says.

The three goddesses smile at Paris.

'**Choose** me,' Hera says, 'and you can be a **great** king of many countries.'

'Choose me,' Athena tells him, 'and you can **win** all **fights** and learn great things.'

'Choose me,' Aphrodite calls, 'and you can marry the most beautiful woman.'

Paris gives the apple to Aphrodite.

At once, Hermes and the three goddesses leave for Mount Olympus.

choose to think which thing you want most

great very important

win to be the best in a fight, or a competition

fight when you hit someone many times; to hit someone again and again

Not long after that, one of King Priam's messengers visits Mount Ida.

'Priam calls all the young men in the country to Troy,' he tells Paris.

'Why?' the young shepherd asks.

'For the **Trojan Games**,' the messenger answers.

So Paris says goodbye to Agelaus and goes to Troy. But the old man goes after him.

~~~~~~~~~~~~

Paris runs very fast and well. He is the best runner in the Trojan Games.

King Priam gives the first **prize** to him.

'What's your name?' the king asks.

'I'm Paris,' the young shepherd answers. 'And I come from Mount Ida.'

Priam suddenly looks at him differently.

'Are you ... my son?' he asks.

Agelaus is standing near them. He quickly tells the king everything.

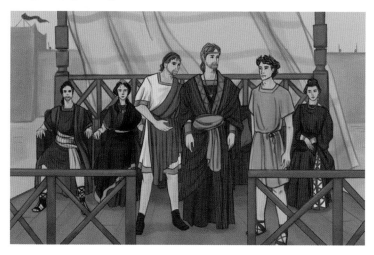

Trojan in, or from, Troy; a person from Troy

Games a very old sports competition for people from different parts of a country

prize a thing that people give you when you are the best at something

9

deed something that you do

Priam is very sorry for his past **deeds**. So he is not angry with Agelaus.

'Paris, my boy, you're alive!' he cries happily. 'You must come home with me.'

So Paris goes and lives in Troy with Priam, Hecuba, Cassandra, and Hector. Then one day, Priam says, 'Son, you must go at once to Sparta, in Greece. You must visit the Spartan king, Menelaus, for me.'

READING CHECK

Put the sentences in order. Number them 1–10.

a ☐ Paris hears about the Trojan Games.

b ☐ Agelaus tells King Priam all about Paris.

c ☐ Hermes and the goddesses take the apple to Mount Ida.

d ☐ Paris goes and lives with Priam and his family.

e ☐ The gods go back to Mount Olympus.

f ☐ Priam gives the first prize to Paris.

g ☐ Priam cries happily because Paris is alive.

h ☐ Paris gives the apple to Aphrodite.

i ☐ Paris tells Priam, 'I'm Paris, from Mount Ida.'

j ☐ Paris goes to Troy and runs in the Games.

GUESS WHAT

What happens in the next chapter? Tick the boxes.   Yes   No

a Paris meets King Menelaus.   ☐   ☐

b Paris meets Menelaus's queen, Helen.   ☐   ☐

c Peleus and Thetis have a son.   ☐   ☐

d Thetis puts her child in the River Styx.   ☐   ☐

e The child dies in the water.   ☐   ☐

f Paris takes Helen home with him to Troy.   ☐   ☐

g Menelaus is angry and speaks to Agamemnon.   ☐   ☐

Chapter 4 Love is beautiful

Paris goes across the sea to Sparta. But old King Menelaus is not there.

'He's in **Mycenae**,' his young queen, Helen, says. 'He's visiting his brother Agamemnon there. Agamemnon is the greatest of all the Greek kings. But please stay here and talk with me.'

Helen is very beautiful, so Paris stays.

〰〰〰〰〰〰〰〰〰

At the same time in Thessaly, King Peleus and Queen Thetis have a son. His name is Achilles.

An old **priestess** tells Thetis, 'You must be careful. One day, your son Achilles must go and fight in Troy. And he must die there, too.'

Mycenae
/ˌmaɪˈsiːni/

priestess a woman who can talk to the gods

Thetis is afraid. She takes Achilles down to the dark **River** Styx. Then she takes her son's left **heel** in her hand. And she puts him under the water for a minute. After this, nobody can kill him with a **sword**. But his left heel stays **weak**.

river a long line of water

heel the back of your foot

sword a long knife for fighting

weak not strong

In Sparta, Paris and Helen talk happily.

'I love you,' Paris says.

'I love you, too,' Helen answers.

'Then come to Troy and marry me,' Paris cries.

'All right,' Helen smiles, and she leaves with him.

When Paris brings Helen of Sparta home, his sister Cassandra is not happy.

'Disaster! Now the Greeks must come for Helen. I see Troy in flames and all our family dead!' she cries. But nobody listens to her.

Paris marries Helen that afternoon. From that day, she is Helen of Troy.

When Menelaus comes back from Mycenae to Sparta, Helen is not at home.

'Where's the queen?' he asks.

He is very angry when he learns. He goes and tells his brother Agamemnon.

'We must fight the Trojans,' Agamemnon cries angrily. 'We must bring Helen back!'

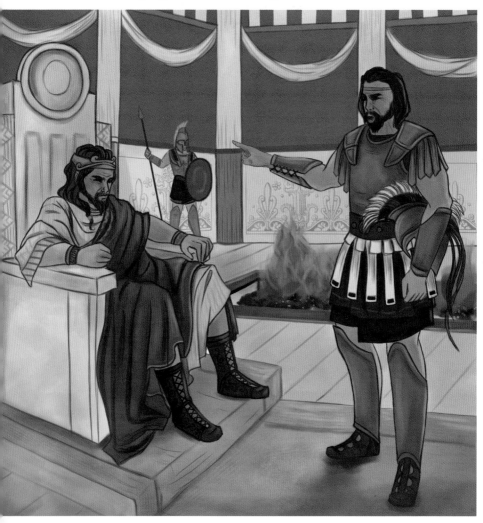

READING CHECK

Correct the mistakes in the sentences.

a Menelaus is in ~~Ithaca~~ *Mycenae* when Paris arrives in Sparta.

b Peleus and Thetis have a son, Patroclus.

c A priestess tells Thetis, 'Your son must die in Thessaly.'

d Thetis puts her child in the River Styx for a day.

e After that, any sword can go through his body.

f But the boy's right heel stays weak.

g Paris takes Thetis home with him to Troy.

h Menelaus is angry when he learns of Hector's visit to Sparta.

i Menelaus goes and speaks with his brother Odysseus.

GUESS WHAT

What happens in the next chapter? Tick two boxes to finish each sentence.

a Paris …
   1 ☐ meets Menelaus and fights him.
   2 ☐ kills Menelaus.
   3 ☐ runs away from Menelaus into Troy.
   4 ☐ dies in Helen's arms.

b Menelaus …
   1 ☐ speaks angrily to Agamemnon about the Trojans.
   2 ☐ fights slowly, but is very strong.
   3 ☐ leaves Troy and goes back to Greece.
   4 ☐ dies with Hector's sword in his back.

15

Chapter 5 Years of war

The Greek fighters are coming across the sea in 1,000 **ships**. The Trojans hear of this and go into Troy. They close the town **gates** and wait for **war**.

After many days at sea, Agamemnon's men arrive on the **beaches** of Troy. That night, they sleep in their **tents** on the beach.

The next day, Menelaus and Odysseus, King of Ithaca, go to the town. They want to speak to King Priam. But the Trojans do not open the gates to them.

Priam's messenger tells the Greeks. 'Helen of Troy is happy here. So leave us, and go home.'

ship you use a ship to go across water

gate a big door into – or out of – a town

war fighting between countries

beach the land next to the sea

tent a house made of cloth that you can take with you when you move

Menelaus and Odysseus go to Agamemnon's tent. They tell the great king everything. He is very angry.

So the Trojan War begins. For years, the Trojans stay in their town. They come out and fight. Then they go back and sleep. For years, the Greeks wait on the beaches. They fight every day, and they eat and drink at night. After many long years, young men are old. Boys are now young men. But the Trojan War doesn't stop.

battle a big fight

One day, Paris and Menelaus meet in **battle**. All the Greek and Trojan fighters watch them. Paris is weaker than Menelaus, but he is faster. In the end, Paris is afraid. He runs away from Menelaus into Troy. The Greeks laugh at him and call him a 'weak boy'. After that, Helen stops speaking to him.

Back in Greece, Achilles is now a young man. With his best friend, Patroclus, he wants to fight the Trojans. But his mother, Thetis, doesn't want to lose him in the war.

ACTIVITIES

READING CHECK

Complete the sentences with the names. You can use each name more than once.

Helen   Paris   Priam   Agamemnon

Menelaus   Odysseus   Thetis   Achilles   Patroclus

a ....Agamemnon... takes 1,000 ships to Troy.

b King .... of Sparta, and King .... of Ithaca go to Troy.

c ....'s messenger speaks to them from the town wall.

d '................. of Troy is happy here,' he tells them.

e They go back to .... and tell him everything.

f One day, old .... and young .... meet in battle.

g .... is afraid and runs away into Troy.

h .... does not speak to .... after that.

i .... and his best friend .... want to fight the Trojans.

j .... does not want to lose her son.

GUESS WHAT

What happens in the next chapter? Match the people with the sentences.

a Achilles ☐

b Hector ☐

c Menelaus ☐

d Odysseus ☐

e Paris ☐

f Priam ☐

1 ... goes to Greece for Achilles.

2 ... kills Patroclus.

3 ... kills Hector.

4 ... asks for his son's dead body.

5 ... kills Achilles.

6 ... finds Helen and takes her back.

19

Chapter 6 When prophecies come true

On the Trojan beach one day, Odysseus asks a **priest**, 'How can we win this war?'

'Bring Achilles here,' the priest answers.

So Odysseus goes to Greece for Achilles.

Before Achilles and Patroclus leave for Troy, Thetis arrives. She gives some golden **armour** to her son.

At first, Achilles does well in Troy. He kills many Trojans. Then he and Agamemnon have a disagreement. Achilles brings back a Trojan woman from one battle. But Agamemnon takes her.

After that, Achilles stays angrily in his tent.

Under Priam's son Hector, the Trojans begin winning the war.

So Patroclus visits Achilles. 'Please come and fight,' he says.

'No,' Achilles answers. But he gives his golden armour to his friend. Patroclus wears it.

In battle, Hector sees the armour. 'Hey, Achilles!' he cries angrily.

Hector fights and kills young Patroclus.

After that, Achilles fights and

priest a man who can talk to the gods

armour when you wear this, people cannot kill you

kills Hector. He takes the Trojan's body back to his tent.

wooden made of wood

That night, Priam comes. He asks for Hector's body. But Achilles says 'no' to him.

Days later, the Greeks get in their ships and go. They leave a big **wooden** horse on the beach. 'What a wonderful horse!' the Trojans cry. They take it into Troy.

arrow you shoot things with this

poison to make someone ill with something bad that you put into their body

prophecy when you say things before they happen

come true to begin to be true

But when the Trojans sleep, the Greek ships come back. Odysseus and his friends come out of the horse. They open the town gates to Agamemnon's men.

Soon Troy is in flames. Trojans and Greeks fight. Paris hits Achilles in the heel with one of his **arrows**. It **poisons** Achilles, and he dies. Then the Greeks kill Priam and Paris. And they find – and take – Hecuba, Cassandra, and Helen. That night, all the different old **prophecies** from before **come true**.

READING CHECK

Choose the correct answers.

a Who does Odysseus speak to?
1 ☑ a priest
2 ☐ Priam

b Who gives armour to Achilles?
1 ☐ Peleus
2 ☐ Thetis

c Who wears Achilles's armour?
1 ☐ Hector
2 ☐ Patroclus

d How do the Greeks get into Troy?
1 ☐ in a wooden horse
2 ☐ under the walls

e What kills Achilles?
1 ☐ an arrow
2 ☐ a sword

GUESS WHAT

What happens after the Greeks take Troy? Choose from these ideas, and write your ideas, too.

a Agamemnon goes home to Mycenae with Cassandra. ☐

b Agamemnon's queen kills him. ☐

c Menelaus and Helen go to Cyprus and Egypt by ship. ☐

d Odysseus goes home to Ithaca, but it takes a long time. ☐

e ....

f ....

Project A *A famous lost city*

1 Read the text about Troy. Use a dictionary to help you. Complete the table below.

Troy is a famous lost city. You can find it at Hisarlık Hill near Çanakkale in north-west Anatolia, in modern-day Turkey. It is an old Hittite city. You can read about it in 'The Iliad', a book by the famous Greek storyteller Homer. This is about the Trojan War. Troy is the home of the Trojan King Priam in that story. These days, you can see a wooden Trojan horse there. Troy is a UNESCO World Heritage site.

What is the name of the city?	
Where is it?	
Which civilization does this city belong to?	
Which famous writer talks about this city and where?	
Which character has his or her home there?	
What can you see there today?	

Read the notes in the table about Carthage and complete the text about it.

What is the name of the city?	Carthage
Where is it?	in Tunis, in modern day Tunisia
Which civilization does this city belong to?	Phoenician
Which famous writer talks about this city and where?	Roman writer Virgil, in his long poem 'The Aeneid' about the Trojan Aeneas's journey from Troy to Italy, and the beginning of the Roman Empire
Which character makes his or her home there?	Carthaginian Queen Dido
What can you see there today?	the ruins of the old Phoenician city

.... is a famous lost city. You can find it in
................., in modern day ....
t is a ....city. You can read about it in the
.... writer ....'s long poem
The Aeneid'. This is about the .... Aeneas, his
ourney from ....to ...., and
he beginning of the ....
.... is the home of the ....
Queen ....in that poem. These days, you
can see the ....of the ....
.... in Tunis.
.... is a UNESCO World Heritage site.

Learn about a different lost city on the Internet. Write a text about it. Use the texts in Activities 1 and 2 to help you.

Mycenae   Petra

Machu Picchu   Persepolis   Xanadu

Project B *Four-word headlines*

Newspaper headlines must be quick and easy to read. They miss out little form words (articles, auxiliary *be*) and use short content words (nouns, verbs, adjectives, adverbs).

1 **Match each four-word headline with the opening sentence of a *Trojan News* story.**

a COUNTRY BOY CHOOSES WINNER

b GODS VISIT KING'S WEDDING

c GREEK FIGHTER'S FRIEND DIES

d KING'S HELPER'S GOOD DEED

e MOTHER AFRAID FOR SON

f *TROJAN LEAVES FIGHT FAST*

1 Priam's young son doesn't like fighting much, but he's very good at running away … ☐

2 The goddess Thetis wants to put her child Achilles in the River Styx … ☐

3 Achilles is very angry tonight because his greatest friend Patroclus is dead … ☐

4 An honest young shepherd must give a prize to the most beautiful goddess today … ☐

5 The king's son isn't dead, but alive on Mount Ida, and we must thank Agelaus for it … ☐

6 Everyone on Mount Olympus wants to be in Thessaly this weekend when Peleus marries sea goddess Thetis … ☐

Match each headline in Activity 1 with a chapter of *Troy*.

Chapter 1: ☐   Chapter 3: ☐   Chapter 5: ☐

Chapter 2: ☐   Chapter 4: ☐   Chapter 6: ☐

Now unjumble the four-word headline for each opening sentence of a new *Trojan News* story.

KING / QUEEN / OLD / LOSES

a King Menelaus's young queen, Helen of Sparta, is now far away in Troy …

APPLE / THREE / WANT / GOLDEN

b Eris's present 'for the most beautiful' brings disagreement between three goddesses at King Peleus's wedding …

SON / PRIZE / WINS / KING'S

c King Priam's youngest son, Paris, is the winner of the first prize in this year's Trojan Games …

GIRL / TROJAN / BATTLE / OVER

d Achilles is not speaking to Agamemnon now the Great King has got the young Trojan woman from Achilles's tent …

Write a new four-word headline for part of the Troy story. Read it aloud. Which part of the story is it from? Your classmates must guess.

WORD WORK 1

1 **These words don't match the pictures. Correct them.**

a ~~queen~~
...........king.........

b king
....

c sheep
....

d shepherd
....

e mountain
....

f heart
....

2 **Complete the sentences with different new words from Chapters 1 and 2.**

a Perhaps Paris can bring d i s a s t e r to Troy.

b In her head, Hecuba sees Troy i _   _ _ a _ e _.

c Paris is very _ o _ e _ _. He always speaks truly.

d Zeus is a Greek _ o _, and Hera is a Greek _ o _ _ e _ _.

e Peleus _ a _ _ ie _ Thetis in Thessaly.

f Peleus and Thetis ask their friends to the _ e _ _ i _ _.

g Eris brings _ i _ a _ _ ee _ e _ _ with her.

h She leaves a _ o _ _ e _ apple on the table.

i Hermes is Zeus's _ e _ _ e _ _ e _. He speaks for Zeus when Zeus is far away.

WORD WORK 2

Find new words from Chapters 3 and 4 in the apples to match the pictures.

a .... heel ....

b ....

c ....

d ....

e ....

f ....

Apples: lehe, tifhg, stepersis, zrepi, drows, verri

Complete each sentence with a word from the box.

| chooses | deeds | Games | greatest | Trojan | weaker | wins |

a Agamemnon is the ...greatest... of all the Greek kings.

b Paris .... the goddess Aphrodite, and he gives the apple to her.

c Priam is the .... king.

d Paris runs very fast in the ....

e Priam speaks to Paris after he .... first prize.

f Priam is not happy about his past ....

g Achilles's left heel is .... than his right heel.

WORD WORK 3

1 Find new words from Chapters 5 and 6 to match the pictures.

a <u>ship</u>   **b** _ _ _ _

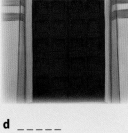

c _ _ _ _ _   **d** _ _ _ _ _   **e** _ _ _ _ _ _

f _ _ _ _ _ _   **g** _ _ _ _ _

2 Correct each underlined word with a new word from Chapters 5 and 6.

a Hecuba and Cassandra's <u>photographs</u> come true. . prophecies.
b The <u>car</u> between Greece and Troy finishes after ten years. ....
c Paris and Menelaus meet in <u>bottle</u>. ....
d The Greeks leave a <u>woman</u> horse behind them. ....
e Don't drink that dirty water. It can <u>person</u> you. ....

GRAMMAR CHECK

Comparative adjectives

We add –er to make the comparative form of most adjectives.

old – older

When adjectives finish in a short vowel and a single consonant, we double the consonant and add –er.

big – bigger

When adjectives finish in consonant + y, we change y to i and add –er.

happy – happier

With longer adjectives (other 2 syllable adjectives, or adjectives with 3+ syllables) we use more.

wonderful – more wonderful

Some adjectives have an irregular comparative form.

bad – worse   good – better

We use comparative adjectives + than in sentences.

Hector is older than Paris.

Write the comparative adjectives.

a young …*younger*…

b honest …………………

c weak …………………

d careful …………………

e hungry …………………

f fast …………………

g angry …………………

h beautiful …………………

i great …………………

Write comparative sentences.

a Paris / young / Cassandra ………*Paris is younger than Cassandra*………

b Patroclus / weak / Achilles …………………………………………………

c Aphrodite / beautiful / Hera …………………………………………………

d Zeus / hungry / Hermes …………………………………………………

e Paris / fast / Menelaus …………………………………………………

f Paris / honest / Agelaus …………………………………………………

g Eris / angry / Athena …………………………………………………

h Agamemnon / great / Menelaus …………………………………………………

i Odysseus / careful / Priam …………………………………………………

GRAMMAR CHECK

Adverbs of manner

We use adverbs of manner to talk about actions. They tell us more about <u>verbs</u>.

Hera <u>looks</u> carefully at the golden apple.   *Achilles <u>fights</u> Hector angrily.*

We make adverbs of manner from adjectives by adding –ly.

careful – carefully

For adjectives ending in –y, we change –y to –ily.

angry – angrily

Some adverbs are irregular.

fast – fast   good – well

I'm King Priam's son, Paris. I love my father greatly. My brother Hector fights well. I fight badly, but I can run fast. I love a wonderful woman – Helen. She speaks beautifully and dresses expensively. But my mother isn't very nice to her. And my sister Cassandra is afraid of her. Cassandra tells me this honestly and openly.

3 Circle the adverbs of manner in the text

4 Choose the correct word to complete each sentence.

a Hecuba is not … with her young son Paris.
   1 ☑ happy   2 ☐ happily

b Priam … gives the child away to Agelaus.
   1 ☐ quick   2 ☐ quickly

c Paris lives … on Mount Ida.
   1 ☐ quiet   2 ☐ quietly

d He is … when the king's messenger visits him.
   1 ☐ excited   2 ☐ excitedly

e Paris wins the Trojan Games … .
   1 ☐ easy   2 ☐ easily

f He finds Helen of Sparta very … .
   1 ☐ interesting   2 ☐ interestingly

GRAMMAR CHECK

Possessive adjectives

We use possessive adjectives to say who something or someone belongs to.

The sea is her home. (= Thetis's)

Paris is his killer. (= Achilles's)

Agamemnon is their great king. (= the Greeks')

Replace the underlined words in these phrases with the possessive adjectives in the box.

her	~~her~~	his	their
its	your	my	our

a Thetis's son ....her............ son

b the wooden horse's legs .... legs

c Achilles's tent .... tent

d Peleus and Thetis's wedding .... wedding

e Athena's father .... father

f 'Achilles's best friend,' Achilles says. '.................. best friend'

g 'Achilles's armour,' Thetis tells Achilles. '.................. armour'

h 'Peleus and Thetis's son,' Peleus and Thetis say. '.................. son'

Complete the sentences with the correct possessive adjectives.

a She goes to the river and puts her son in ....its........ waters.

b No one can put a sword through Achilles's body now, but .... heel stays weak.

c Cassandra is angry when .... brother brings Helen home.

d '.................. wife is in Troy now,' Menelaus tells .... brother.

e The Greeks go in .... ships across the sea.

f 'Give .... black arrows to me!' Paris tells Priam.

g Cassandra loses .... father, and .... brothers in the war.

Dominoes is an enjoyable series of illustrated classic and modern stories in four carefully graded language stages – from Starter to Three – which take learners from beginner to intermediate level.

Each *Domino* reader includes:
- a good story to read and enjoy
- integrated activities to develop reading skills and increase active vocabulary
- personalized projects to make the language and story themes more meaningful
- contextualized grammar practice.

Each *Domino* pack contains a reader, plus a MultiROM with:
- a complete audio recording of the story, fully dramatized to bring it to life
- interactive activities to offer further practice in reading and language skills and to consolidate learning.

If you liked this Quick Starter Level *Domino*, why not read these?

Crying Wolf and Other Tales
Aesop

'Help! A wolf is eating my sheep!'

What happens when a bored shepherd boy lies to the people in his village – or when he later tells the truth?

What do a man and his wife do when their goose lays golden eggs? And what can two travellers learn from a bear in the woods?

These three old Greek tales teach us important truths about people today!

Book ISBN: 978 0 19 424971 3
MultiROM Pack ISBN: 978 0 19 424953 9

The Sorcerer's Apprentice

'What's your job?' Yukio asks.

'I'm a sorcerer,' the old man smiles. 'And I need a young apprentice.'

One day Yukio – a young boy from old Japan – leaves his sister in the country and looks for a job in the town. He finds interesting work there: being a sorcerer's apprentice. But why must Yukio wait to learn magic? And what happens after he puts a spell on a broom when the sorcerer is away?

Book ISBN: 978 0 19 424976 8
MultiROM Pack ISBN: 978 0 19 424960 7

You can find details and a full list of books in the Oxford Graded Readers catalogue and Oxford English Language Teaching Catalogue, and on the website: www.oup.com/elt

Teachers: see www.oup.com/elt for a full range of online support, or consult your local office.

	CEFR	Cambridge Exams	IELTS	TOEFL iBT	TOEIC
Level 3	B1	PET	4.0	57-86	550
Level 2	A2–B1	KET-PET	3.0-4.0	–	–
Level 1	A1–A2	YLE Flyers/KET	3.0	–	–
Starter & Quick Starter	A1	YLE Movers	–	–	–